'Go away and find some news,' says Mr Frank to Mike. 'This is your last chance.'

Mike is a good cameraman but his boss at SFX news, Mr Frank, doesn't think so. Mike has a nice life and he needs his job. What can he do?

In Hawaii a volcano is erupting – a good chance for a good story. Mike goes there to film the story, but it is dangerous on the volcano and he learns that some things are more important than his job, or his camera.

This really is his last chance . . .

OXFORD BOOKWORMS LIBRARY
Thriller & Adventure

Last Chance

Starter (250 headwords)

PHILLIP BURROWS AND MARK FOSTER

Last Chance

OXFORD UNIVERSITY PRESS

OXFORD

UNIVERSITY PRESS

Great Clarendon Street, Oxford OX2 6DP

Oxford University Press is a department of the University of Oxford.
It furthers the University's objective of excellence in research, scholarship,
and education by publishing worldwide in

Oxford New York

Auckland Cape Town Dar es Salaam Hong Kong Karachi
Kuala Lumpur Madrid Melbourne Mexico City Nairobi
New Delhi Shanghai Taipei Toronto

With offices in

Argentina Austria Brazil Chile Czech Republic France Greece
Guatemala Hungary Italy Japan Poland Portugal Singapore
South Korea Switzerland Thailand Turkey Ukraine Vietnam

OXFORD and OXFORD ENGLISH are registered trade marks of
Oxford University Press in the UK and in certain other countries

© Oxford University Press 2008

The moral rights of the author have been asserted

Database right Oxford University Press (maker)

10

ISBN: 978 0 19 423436 8

A complete recording of this Bookworms edition of *Last Chance*
is available on audio CD ISBN: 978 0 19 423437 5

Printed in China

Word count (main text): 1928

For more information on the Oxford Bookworms Library,
visit www.oup.com/bookworms

CONTENTS

LAST CHANCE

'Come in here!' says Mike's boss. He is angry – again.

Mike is a cameraman and he works for SFX News. His boss, Mr Frank, is angry with him. It is the second time this week.

Mike walks slowly into the office. He is in big trouble.

'Close the door,' says Mr Frank. There is a video in his hand.

'This is bad,' thinks Mike. 'He doesn't like my work.'

1

Mr Frank looks at Mike. 'Are you a news cameraman?' he asks.

'Yes, of course,' says Mike.

'Well, this isn't news.' He throws the video at the door. 'It's . . . it's . . . I have a three-year-old son. He can do better. Go away and find some news. I want a film that hits me here.' Mr Frank puts his hand on his heart.

'And Mike . . .'

'Yes, Boss?'

'This is your last chance.'

Mike walks slowly out of Mr Frank's office. His face is red.

'He can't talk to me like that,' he thinks. 'I'm a good cameraman. I'm unlucky, that's all. But I can't be angry with him because I need my job.'

Mike sits on his chair and looks out of the window. He sees an old man sitting in his garden. He feels tired. 'Am I too old for this job?' thinks Mike. 'Am I too tired?'

There is a newspaper on Mike's desk. He picks it up and reads it. There is a volcano in Hawaii. The volcano is erupting and people are leaving. Mike sees a photograph of the volcano. It looks dangerous. 'Hmm. Maybe . . .' he thinks.

Mr Frank walks past. 'Reading the newspaper?' he says. 'Remember – this is your last chance.'

Mike feels very angry but he says nothing. 'This is bad,' he thinks. 'I must go to Hawaii and make an exciting film.'

4

Mike gets in his car and quickly drives home. He has a nice car. It is fast and he loves it. It is also expensive. He needs to work.

Mike stops the car next to his house. He goes in the house. 'What do I need?' he thinks. He puts some clothes in a bag and picks it up.

'One more thing,' he thinks. 'My video camera.' He picks up his camera and gives it a kiss. 'We can do it, old friend,' he says.

Later that day, Mike takes a plane to Hawaii. There are only seven people on the plane. He looks out of the window. 'Hawaii is beautiful!' he thinks. There are big waves on the sea. 'I would like to go surfing,' thinks Mike. 'Perhaps another time.'

But as the plane gets closer, the sky is very dark.

At the airport lots of people are running. Some people are crying. 'The volcano is erupting,' they say to Mike. 'Why are you here?'

'I'm here because I'm a news cameraman. A *good* news cameraman,' he tells them. He can see the volcano. It is a long way away. There is black smoke and red fire. 'Is this a good idea?' thinks Mike.

Some news people are leaving Hawaii. They are getting on a plane. Mike talks to them. A girl tells him that the volcano is very dangerous.

'I think my friend Jenny is there. She wants to make a film, too. Is she alive or dead? I don't know,' says the girl. 'You must come with us,' she says, 'You can't go to the volcano.'

'I want to leave the island,' thinks Mike. 'I don't want to die, but . . .'

'I can't go with you. I have work to do,' he says.

'OK,' says the girl. 'Look out for my friend Jenny. She has big blue eyes. Please tell her to leave the island.'

'OK,' says Mike. He says goodbye to the girl. He watches the plane leave. 'This really is my last chance,' he thinks.

Just then the volcano makes a big noise. A dog runs quickly past. An old woman starts to cry. Mike looks at her. He wants to say something but he can't. The sun is hot but suddenly he is cold. He is afraid.

'I can't be afraid,' he says. He looks at his camera and says, 'Let's go, old friend.'

Mike walks through the town. The sky is getting darker. The red fire over the volcano is getting bigger and bigger. Mike is feeling more afraid.

In the town Mike meets a man. The man is leaving with his family. 'How can I get to the volcano?' Mike asks.

'Cars don't go to the volcano,' says the man. 'The drivers are afraid. You must walk.'

'Is it far?' asks Mike.

'No,' says the man. 'But the fire is hot. Take lots of water with you.'

There is a television in a shop window. It is not showing pictures of the volcano. 'I am the only news person here,' Mike thinks. 'I have a chance to make the only film about the volcano. I must go.'

The road in front of him is very long. His legs feel tired but he begins to walk.

After two long hours, Mike is on the volcano. There is a lot of smoke and a lot of fire. Mike can't see any people.

'I must be quick,' he thinks. Mike films the smoke and the fire. A big rock nearly hits him but he films it. 'This film is good,' he thinks.

He is afraid but happy. 'How can Mr Frank be angry now?' Mike thinks. He is taking lots of film.

Another rock almost hits him. Mike feels hot and tired.
'It's time to go,' says Mike. 'Good job!' he says to his
camera.

A bigger rock goes over his head. 'I don't like this. I
must go now,' he says. Mike can smell the smoke. He can
feel the fire.

Mike puts his camera under his arm. He starts to run. Just then the volcano makes a noise. Mike runs faster. Suddenly, he hears a different noise.

'Is that a woman?' thinks Mike. 'It can't be. There is nobody here.'

He starts to run again, but then . . .

'Help!'

'It *is* somebody. They need me,' he thinks. 'Hello,' he says. 'Where are you?' Mike looks everywhere, but he can't see anybody.

'I'm here. Please help me!'

Mike sees something behind a rock. It moves. He goes to the rock and sees a young woman there. She can't move her leg because it is under the rock.

'Oh, thank you. Thank you,' she says to Mike. She begins to cry. 'My leg. I think it's broken.'

'Wait a minute,' says Mike. 'I can help.'

He pushes the rock. It is too big. There are small rocks in front. He pushes them away then pushes the big rock again. It moves a little. He pushes harder. It moves a little more.

'Aargh,' cries the woman.

Suddenly the rock moves down the volcano.

The woman's face is white. She smiles slowly.

'Are you Jenny?' Mike asks.

'Yes, I am!' she says. 'How do you know?'

'It doesn't matter now. My name is Mike. I have to carry you, Jenny. But first . . .'

Mike has a tripod. He ties it to Jenny's leg. 'Does that feel better?' he asks.

Jenny smiles again. 'Thank you, Mike,' she says. She is very tired. 'I'm usually very careful – but not today.'

'Come on. We have to get off the volcano,' says Mike.

'Put your arm around me,' Mike tells Jenny. He puts down his camera. Jenny gets up slowly. Her leg is very bad.

'Take it easy,' Mike says. They start to walk very slowly.

'It's okay,' he says. 'You're okay.'

Metre by metre they move down the volcano. They are almost hit by rocks. Black smoke is in their mouths. Hot fire is close behind them. But they are alive.

'Mike – wait,' says Jenny suddenly. 'Your camera!' She stops walking. Her face is black with smoke. Jenny's blue eyes look at Mike.

Mike looks back at Jenny. 'You're more important than my camera,' he tells her.

'But the volcano . . . I can wait here. You go back. It's not too late.'

Mike says nothing.

They keep walking slowly down the volcano – and away from Mike's camera.

Jenny is now very tired. Her leg is badly broken. Mike stops behind a big rock.

'Do you want some water?' he asks.

Mike has some water in his bag. Jenny and Mike are both thirsty. They drink the water.

Jenny begins to go to sleep. 'This is dangerous. Jenny must stay alive,' Mike thinks. 'Don't go to sleep, Jenny. Talk to me. Where is your home? Tell me about your family. Do you like books?'

They walk and Jenny talks. When she stops talking, Mike asks another question.

They are almost off the volcano. Mike looks back. Where is his camera? Is it in the fire?

They are off the volcano. Mike sits down next to Jenny.
He puts his head in his hands.

'What's the matter?' asks Jenny.

'Everything,' says Mike. 'I have no camera and no film.
Now I don't have a job. There are no more chances.'

Jenny puts her arm around him. 'It's okay.'

Two hours later, they walk into the town. People come out to see them.

'Are you all right?' they ask Jenny.

'I have a broken leg, but I am alive,' she says, and looks at Mike. 'Thank you, Mike.' He smiles.

'There is a helicopter waiting for you,' says a man in a suit. 'It is leaving the island. You must get on quickly.' The man helps them into the helicopter.

In the helicopter, a man says to Mike, 'Do you need anything?'

'My camera,' he says. 'But it is on the volcano. My camera is my best friend and oldest friend.' Mike closes his eyes and goes to sleep.

Mike is now at home. He does not want to see his boss, Mr Frank. Then one morning he hears the telephone. 'Hello?' he says.

'This is Mr Frank. You must come to work tomorrow. I need to talk to you. Goodbye.'

The next day, Mike goes to work. His friends are happy to see him. 'Well done, Mike,' they say.

'Thanks,' says Mike. He is happy to see his friends, but he is afraid of Mr Frank.

His boss sees him. 'You, get in here.'

'This is it,' thinks Mike.

In the office Mr Frank looks at Mike. He has something in his hands. 'Do you remember the people in the helicopter?' he asks.

'Yes,' says Mike.

'They remember you. I think you need to thank them.' He moves his hands. There is Mike's camera.

'My camera!' says Mike.

'The camera is broken,' says Mr Frank, 'But we have the film and it's very good.' He smiles.

'My old friend,' says Mike to his camera. He gives it a kiss.

'Let's watch your video,' Mr Frank says.

They watch the film on the TV. They can see Mike and Jenny. Mike moves the big rock. He helps Jenny to walk. Big rocks are falling out of the sky. The volcano makes a noise. The fire is red and the smoke is black. It is very exciting.

'Next time, remember to turn it off. Or maybe not!' says Mr Frank. 'This video hits me . . . right here!'

Then Mr Frank says, 'Oh, and Mike – we have a new news person.'

Jenny comes into the room. She isn't black with smoke now. She smiles at Mike. 'She's beautiful,' Mike thinks. 'She hits me . . . right here!'

GLOSSARY

around all the way round

boss a person who tells workers what to do

broken in pieces or not working

camera a thing you use for taking photographs or
moving pictures

cameraman a person who films

carry to take

chance when something can happen

dangerous that can kill you

erupt to throw out gas, hot rocks, and liquid rocks

exciting making you feel very happy

film (*v*) to use cameras to make a movie; (*n*) moving
pictures that tell a story

idea something that you think

job work

kiss (*v*) to touch lovingly with your mouth

surfing standing or lying on a flat board when the sea
carries you back to the beach

throw to make something move from your hand through
the air

trouble problems

unlucky when something bad happens to you

volcano a mountain with a hole in the top where fire,
gas, and hot liquid rock sometimes come out

Last Chance

ACTIVITIES

Before Reading

1 **Look at the front cover of the book. Answer these questions.**

1 The main character in the story is …

a ☐ a gardener

b ☐ a student

c ☐ a cameraman

2 The story happens …

a ☐ in an office

b ☐ in an airport

c ☐ on a volcano

2 **Read the back cover of the book. Answer these questions.**

1 How will the story make you feel?

a ☐ Happy

b ☐ Sad

c ☐ Excited

2 Who has one 'last chance'?

a ☐ Mr Frank

b ☐ Mike

c ☐ Jenny

While Reading

1 Read pages 1–5. Now answer these questions.

1 Where is the volcano?
2 What is the name of Mike's boss?
3 What is Mike's job?
4 What does Mike see through the window?
5 Mike's boss has a son. How old is he?
6 Is Mike happy?

2 Read pages 6–9. Now make these sentences correct.

1 There are only three people on the plane.
2 There are big birds on the sea.
3 A girl tells him that the volcano is very beautiful.
4 Her friend has big green eyes.

3 Read pages 10–13. Put these sentences in the correct order. Number them 1–4.

a ☐ Mike starts to run away.
b ☐ Mike hears someone shout, 'Help!'
c ☐ A man says Mike must walk to the volcano.
d ☐ A big rock nearly hits Mike.

30

4 Read pages 14–17. Now answer these questions.

Who …

1 … says, 'Take it easy.'?

2 … has a white face?

What …

3 … is on Jenny's leg?

4 … does Mike tie to Jenny's leg?

5 Read pages 18–21. Now answer these questions.

1 Why is Mike unhappy?

a ☐ Because he has a bad leg.

b ☐ Because he doesn't want to leave the volcano.

c ☐ Because he doesn't have his camera.

2 What does Mike have in his bag?

a ☐ A sandwich.

b ☐ A menu.

c ☐ Some water.

6 Before you read pages 22–24, what do you think happens?

	Yes	No
1 Jenny finds Mike's camera.	☐	☐
2 Mr Frank is pleased with Mike.	☐	☐
3 Mike loses his job.	☐	☐
4 Mike kisses his camera.	☐	☐
5 Mike kisses Jenny.	☐	☐

After Reading

1 **What do you know about Mike? Write about him using these words:**

job / cameraman / good
boss / nasty / afraid
drive / car / fast
best friend / camera
like surfing

2 **Make four complete sentences. Use these words:**

and / but / when / because

1 Mike loses his camera …
2 Mike pushes the rock …
3 Mr Frank is angry …
4 The volcano erupts …

a) … black smoke comes out of the top.
b) … he helps Jenny on the volcano.
c) … it is too big too move.
d) … Mike is reading the newspaper.

3 Who says these words? Who do they say it to?

1 'This is your last chance.'

2 'We can do it, old friend.'

3 'Look out for my friend Jenny.'

4 'Take lots of water with you.'

5 'I'm here. Please help me!'

6 'Don't go to sleep, Jenny.'

4 Complete this summary of the story. Use these words:

boss / like / job / Jenny / volcano / rock
helicopter / hears / camera / chance

Mike is in trouble because his _____ does not
_____ his work. Mr Frank gives Mike one last
_____ .

He goes to Hawaii to film a _____ . He _____
a woman shout 'Help!' when he is filming. The woman is
called _____ . Her leg is under a _____ . Mike
moves the rock and carries her down the volcano, but he
loses his _____ . He thinks he will lose his job too. But
a _____ finds his camera and the film is very good.
Mike's boss is very happy. Mike is also happy when Jenny
gets a _____ working with him.

ABOUT THE AUTHORS

Mark Foster and Phillip Burrows have worked as a writer/ illustrator team since 1991. They were born three years and many miles apart, but they are very nearly twins. They drive the same car, work on the same computers, and wear the same wellington boots – but not at the same time! They spend all the money they get from writing on gadgets, but please don't tell their wives. Mark and Phill have worked together on several Bookworms, including *Taxi of Terror* and *Orca* (Starter). When they meet to write, they like to go to expensive hotels, eat chips dipped in coffee, and laugh at their own jokes.

OXFORD BOOKWORMS LIBRARY

Classics • Crime & Mystery • Factfiles • Fantasy & Horror
Human Interest • Playscripts • Thriller & Adventure
True Stories • World Stories

The OXFORD BOOKWORMS LIBRARY provides enjoyable reading in English, with a wide range of classic and modern fiction, non-fiction, and plays. It includes original and adapted texts in seven carefully graded language stages, which take learners from beginner to advanced level. An overview is given on the next pages.

All Stage 1 titles are available as audio recordings, as well as over eighty other titles from Starter to Stage 6. All Starters and many titles at Stages 1 to 4 are specially recommended for younger learners. Every Bookworm is illustrated, and Starters and Factfiles have full-colour illustrations.

The OXFORD BOOKWORMS LIBRARY also offers extensive support. Each book contains an introduction to the story, notes about the author, a glossary, and activities. Additional resources include tests and worksheets, and answers for these and for the activities in the books. There is advice on running a class library, using audio recordings, and the many ways of using Oxford Bookworms in reading programmes. Resource materials are available on the website <www.oup.com/bookworms>.

The *Oxford Bookworms Collection* is a series for advanced learners. It consists of volumes of short stories by well-known authors, both classic and modern. Texts are not abridged or adapted in any way, but carefully selected to be accessible to the advanced student.

You can find details and a full list of titles in the *Oxford Bookworms Library Catalogue* and *Oxford English Language Teaching Catalogues*, and on the website <www.oup.com/bookworms>.

THE OXFORD BOOKWORMS LIBRARY
GRADING AND SAMPLE EXTRACTS

STARTER • 250 HEADWORDS

present simple – present continuous – imperative –
can/cannot, must – going to (future) – simple gerunds ...

Her phone is ringing – but where is it?

Sally gets out of bed and looks in her bag. No phone.
She looks under the bed. No phone. Then she looks
behind the door. There is her phone. Sally picks up her
phone and answers it. ***Sally's Phone***

STAGE 1 • 400 HEADWORDS

... past simple – coordination with *and*, *but*, *or* –
subordination with *before*, *after*, *when*, *because*, *so* ...

I knew him in Persia. He was a famous builder and I
worked with him there. For a time I was his friend, but
not for long. When he came to Paris, I came after him –
I wanted to watch him. He was a very clever, very
dangerous man. ***The Phantom of the Opera***

STAGE 2 • 700 HEADWORDS

... present perfect – *will* (future) – *(don't) have to, must not, could* –
comparison of adjectives – simple *if* clauses – past continuous –
tag questions – *ask/tell* + infinitive ...

While I was writing these words in my diary, I decided
what to do. I must try to escape. I shall try to get down
the wall outside. The window is high above the ground,
but I have to try. I shall take some of the gold with me – if
I escape, perhaps it will be helpful later. ***Dracula***

STAGE 3 • 1000 HEADWORDS

... should, may – present perfect continuous – *used to* – past perfect
– causative – relative clauses – indirect statements ...

Of course, it was most important that no one should see Colin, Mary, or Dickon entering the secret garden. So Colin gave orders to the gardeners that they must all keep away from that part of the garden in future. ***The Secret Garden***

STAGE 4 • 1400 HEADWORDS

*... past perfect continuous – passive (simple forms) –
would* conditional clauses – indirect questions –
relatives with *where/when* – gerunds after prepositions/phrases ...

I was glad. Now Hyde could not show his face to the world again. If he did, every honest man in London would be proud to report him to the police. ***Dr Jekyll and Mr Hyde***

STAGE 5 • 1800 HEADWORDS

... future continuous – future perfect –
passive (modals, continuous forms) –
would have conditional clauses – modals + perfect infinitive ...

If he had spoken Estella's name, I would have hit him. I was so angry with him, and so depressed about my future, that I could not eat the breakfast. Instead I went straight to the old house. ***Great Expectations***

STAGE 6 • 2500 HEADWORDS

... passive (infinitives, gerunds) – advanced modal meanings –
clauses of concession, condition

When I stepped up to the piano, I was confident. It was as if I knew that the prodigy side of me really did exist. And when I started to play, I was so caught up in how lovely I looked that I didn't worry how I would sound. ***The Joy Luck Club***

Escape

PHILLIP BURROWS AND MARK FOSTER

'I'm not a thief. I'm an innocent man,' shouts Brown. He is angry because he is in prison and the prison guards hate him. Then one day Brown has an idea. It is dangerous – very dangerous.

Orca

PHILLIP BURROWS AND MARK FOSTER

When Tonya and her friends decide to sail around the world they want to see exciting things and visit exciting places.

But one day, they meet an orca – a killer whale – one of the most dangerous animals in the sea. And life gets a little too exciting.

Taxi of Terror

PHILLIP BURROWS AND MARK FOSTER

'How does it work?' Jack asks when he opens his present – a mobile phone. Later that night, Jack is a prisoner in a taxi in the empty streets of the dark city. He now tries his mobile phone for the first time. Can it save his life?

Drive into Danger

ROSEMARY BORDER

'I can drive a truck,' says Kim on her first day at work in the office. When Kim's passenger Andy finds something strange under the truck things get dangerous – very dangerous.

Star Reporter

JOHN ESCOTT

'There's a new girl in town,' says Joe, and soon Steve is out looking for her. Marietta is easy to find in a small town, but every time he sees her something goes wrong . . . and his day goes from bad to worse.

Give us the Money

MAEVE CLARKE

'Every day is the same. Nothing exciting ever happens to me,' thinks Adam one boring Monday morning. But today is not the same. When he helps a beautiful young woman because some men want to take her bag, life gets exciting and very, very dangerous.